THE STORY OF MARTIN MILLER'S GIN

THE STORY OF MARTIN MILLER'S GIN

PRINTED BY UNIPRINT AS
TYPESET IN VENETIAN AND SHARNEY
FIRST PUBLISHED SEPTEMBER 2008

COPYRIGHT & PUBLISHED BY
PAPYRUS INVESTMENTS LTD.
ST HELIER, JERSEY, JE4 5PS
UNITED KINGDOM

LOVE

OBSESSION

AND

SOME DEGREE OF MADNESS...

MARTIN MILLERS'S GIN 1998 - 2008

THE STORY OF MARTIN MILLER'S GIN

THE STORY OF MARTIN MILLER'S GIN

LOVE

A TALE OF THREE MEN, A BAR AND A BAD GIN AND TONIC.

PICTURE A QUIET BAR IN NOTTING HILL GATE SOME TIME IN THE LATE SUMMER OF 1998. THREE FRIENDS ARE SITTING AROUND THREE VERY SAD LOOKING GIN AND TONICS. ONE OF THEM, A CERTAIN MARTIN MILLER, SITS, STIRRING HIS MELTING ICE, QUIETLY MURMURING TO HIMSELF. PUSHING AWAY HIS DRINK, HE LOOKS UP AND ASKS, "YOU KNOW WHAT I'M GOING TO DO?" "NO." REPLY HIS TWO FRIENDS. "I'M GOING TO MAKE MY OWN GIN." "WHAT ON EARTH HAVE YOU BEEN DRINKING?" THEY ASK, (THEY'VE HEARD THIS SORT OF THING FROM HIM BEFORE). IN REPLY MARTIN FIRES A QUESTION BACK AT THEM. "JUST SUPPOSE TIME AND MONEY WERE NO OBJECT, WHAT WOULD IT TAKE FOR US TO MAKE THE PERFECT GIN?" HIS FRIENDS SIMPLY SHRUGGED. "WELL, DO YOU WANT TO KNOW WHAT I THINK?" THEY KNEW THEY WOULD HAVE NO CHOICE IN THE MATTER. "WELL GIN CERTAINLY SHOULDN'T TASTE LIKE THIS," HE SAID, WRINKLING HIS NOSE, "ISN'T GIN SUPPOSED TO TASTE GOOD? NO, NOT JUST GOOD, GREAT; EVEN WHEN DRUNK NEAT." HE WAS NOW TOYING WITH A LIMP LEMON SLICE, SPEARING IT ABSENTMINDEDLY WITH THE END OF A COCKTAIL STICK. "AFTER ALL GIN ISN'T SOME BORING NEUTRAL SPIRIT; GIN IS THE MOST SEDUCTIVE OF DRINKS. GOOD GIN SHOULD SIMPLY INVITE YOU TO LOVE IT." HE WAS WARMING TO THE SUBJECT. "THINK OF IT THIS WAY," HE CONTINUED, "GIN IS LIKE HISTORY IN A GLASS. GIN HAS CREATED SOCIAL REVOLUTIONS; MADE LAWS AND BROKEN LAWS. IT SIMPLY WOULDN'T EXIST IF MARCO POLO AND THOSE EARLY TRAVELLERS HADN'T FOLLOWED THE SILK ROAD." HE PAUSED FOR A SECOND, "OR, FOR THAT MATTER, SUPPOSE COLUMBUS HADN'T SET OUT IN SEARCH OF THE INDIES AND GOT HIMSELF HOPELESSLY LOST IN THE AMERICAS, ALSO NO GIN." "NO," HE STATED FIRMLY, "IT'S NOT JUST HISTORY IN A GLASS, IT'S ROMANCE AND ADVENTURE TOO." PEERING INTO HIS OWN GLASS, HE ENQUIRED OF HIS FRIENDS, "COME ON TELL ME, WHERE'S THE ROMANCE IN VODKA?" BEFORE THEY COULD OPEN THEIR MOUTHS HE HAD HIS OWN ANSWER. "VODKA'S A MEDICINE NOT A DRINK; A TRIUMPH OF SCIENCE OVER THE HEART." HE LOOKED UP AT HIS FRIENDS AND ENQUIRED, "COME ON, WHERE'S THE LOVE IN THAT?" HIS FRIENDS SIMPLY TURNED THEIR EYES TO THE HEAVENS.

"Martin Miller's people are people who seek change, people who are looking for something new and authentic, but don't like the transience of fashion. After all, styles will always change, but good taste remains the same."
MARTIN MILLER

THE STORY OF MARTIN MILLER'S GIN

OBSESSION

GIN FROM THE HEART

"BUT WHAT'S NEW THAT WE CAN BRING TO THE TABLE?" ASKED ONE OF HIS FRIENDS. "DON'T GINS NEED SOME SORT OF GIMMICK OR SECRET INGREDIENT?" SAID THE OTHER. MARTIN PRACTICALLY EXPLODED.

"DON'T YOU UNDERSTAND WHAT I'M TALKING ABOUT?", HE ROARED (NEVER ONE TO SUFFER FOOLS GLADLY).

"MY AIM ISN'T TO CREATE SOME ECCENTRIC 'FLASH IN THE PAN' GIN, SCENTED LIKE SOME OLD LADIES BOUDOIR! I WANT TO CREATE A MODERN CLASSIC, A GIN FOR EVERYONE WHO CAN APPRECIATE FINE GIN."

"AS I'VE SAID BEFORE," HE CONTINUED MORE PATIENTLY, "GIN BY ITS NATURE, HAS TO BE SEDUCTIVE AND I WANT MY GIN TO BE THE MOST SEDUCTIVE OF ALL."

HE SNATCHED A NAPKIN AND STARTED TO SCRIBBLE A LIST. "WE WILL SOURCE JUNIPER FROM TUSCANY AND INDIA, CASSIA BARK FROM CHINA, SCOUR FRANCE FOR THE BEST ANGELICA, AND GET OUR FLORENTINE IRIS FROM, WELL, FLORENCE." LOOKING UP HE CONTINUED, "I'M TELLING YOU, MY GIN IS GOING TO SMELL OF ORIENTAL FLOWERS AT DUSK AND HAVE THE FRAGRANCE OF ORANGE GROVES ON A WARM NIGHT IN SEVILLE." HE LOOKED DREAMILY AT NO ONE IN PARTICULAR AND MURMERED, "AND I WANT IT TO WHISPER TO ME OF CLEAN STANDS OF FIR TREES IN THE WINTER WIND." HIS FRIENDS LOOKED AT EACH OTHER BEMUSED AS HE RE-READ HIS NAPKIN, TICKING EACH DETAIL OFF HIS LIST IN AN EXAGGERATED MANNER.

"AND THE DISTILLATION? HOW ABOUT THAT?" ASKED ONE. HE CAME BACK IMMEDIATELY. "ISN'T IT OBVIOUS? WE WILL FIND THE BEST DISTILLER IN ENGLAND AND DEMAND HE USES ONLY THE MOST TRADITONAL METHODS. NO NEW FANGLED BERRY TRAYS OR CARTERHEADS FOR US." HE TURNED UP HIS NOSE IN DISGUST AT THE THOUGHT.

"I WILL INSIST ON A DISTILLER'S CUT, STRAIGHT FROM THE HEART OF THE SPIRIT, SHARP AS A SAVILE ROW SUIT, YET AS SMOOTH AND REFINED AS THAT CLASSIC BENTLEY I USED TO OWN." HE WAS NOW CHUCKLING TO HIMSELF.

"THAT'S IT. I WANT TO CREATE A MODERN CLASSIC, BUT WITH A TWIST ON TRADITION, IT'LL BE A FRESH, SOFT GIN UNLIKE ANY OTHER." HE THOUGHT FOR A SECOND, THEN, WITH A FINAL FLOURISH, HE CONCLUDED,

"OUR OBSESSIVE ATTENTION TO EVERY LAST DETAIL, THAT WILL BE OUR SECRET INGREDIENT!"

"I'm no master distiller - passion, curiousity, obsession, and blind stubborness gave me what I wanted to achieve. I guess I just followed my instincts."
MARTIN MILLER

THE STORY OF MARTIN MILLER'S GIN

THE STORY OF MARTIN MILLER'S GIN

AND SOME DEGREE OF MADNESS...

DOES DISTANCE REALLY LEND ENCHANTMENT?

"OF COURSE, THE SECRET MAY ALSO BE IN THE WATER"
SAID MARTIN, BREAKING THE SILENCE AT LAST.
"WHAT DO YOU MEAN? WHAT SECRET?"
"ALL OTHER GINS USE DEMINERALIZED WATER."
HIS FRIENDS LOOKED NONPLUSSED.
"WELL YES, AND SO WHAT?" THEY SAID.
"DO YOU KNOW WHAT ICELANDERS CALL
DEMINERALIZED WATER? DEAD WATER. THAT'S WHAT,"
HE ANSWERED ON THEIR BEHALF.
"DEAD?" THEY LOOKED BLANK. "HOW DEAD?"
"WELL, THEY BELIEVE THAT BY PROCESSING OR
DE-MINERALISING WATER IT LOSES SOMETHING,
ITS LIFE FORCE."
"LIFE FORCE?" THEY LOOKED AT HIM DUBIOUSLY.
"YES." HE SAID, THEN, AS IF TALKING TO A CHILD,
"ICELANDERS, TO THIS DAY, BELIEVE ELVES AND SPIRITS
LIVE IN ALL THINGS, THEY CALL THEM 'THE HIDDEN
PEOPLE' AND THEY BELIEVE THEY IMPART LIFE TO THE
NATURAL WORLD. THEY ARE TREATED WITH GREAT
RESPECT. THEY LIVE IN ROCKS, CAVES, AND IN WATER
OF COURSE." BOTH FRIENDS LOOKED INCREDULOUS.

"LOOK," HE SAID, "IT'S NOT THE ONLY REASON WHY WE
MUST USE THIS WATER. NOT ONLY IS IT THE PUREST
WATER ON EARTH, IT'S ALSO THE SOFTEST."
HE LOOKED AT THEM, EXPECTING THE PENNY TO DROP,
BUT THEY STILL DIDN'T SEEM THAT CONVINCED.
"THINK OF IT THIS WAY THEN. IMAGINE WATER THAT FELL
AS RAIN WHEN THE EARTH WAS A YOUNGER AND LESS
POLLUTED PLANET, NOW THINK OF THAT SAME RAIN
TAKING MILLENNIA TO FILTER THROUGH HUNDREDS OF
FEET OF LAVA TO CREATE WATER OF UNRIVALLED PURITY
AND SOFTNESS; WHAT'S MORE, IT'S SIMPLY PERFECT FOR
BLENDING GIN."
SMILING TO HIMSELF HE CONTINUED, "SO IF YOU EVER
NEED PROOF THAT DISTANCE LENDS ENCHANTMENT,
ONE TASTE OF MARTIN MILLER'S SHOULD DO IT."
NOW HE WAS GRINNING LIKE A CHESHIRE CAT,
"MARTIN MILLER'S - THE MOST ENCHANTING OF GINS."
"SO YOU'RE GOING TO SEND THE GIN 1500 MILES JUST
TO ADD WATER?" ASKED HIS FRIENDS IN DISBELIEF.
"YES," HE RETORTED WITHOUT HESITATION.
"YOU'RE MAD," THEY ANSWERED, "LET'S DO IT."

"I suppose it depends on the object and the distance."
MARTIN MILLER

THE STORY OF MARTIN MILLER'S GIN

"Style changes, good taste remains the same"
MARTIN MILLER

THE STORY OF MARTIN MILLER'S GIN

ENGLAND DISTILLED

THE STORY OF MARTIN MILLER'S GIN

THE STORY OF MARTIN MILLER'S GIN

THE FOUR MAIN THINGS

SIMPLY PUT, GIN IS PURE ALCOHOL THAT HAS BEEN FLAVOURED. THE FLAVOUR COMES FROM JUNIPER BERRIES, AND SUCH SUBTLE ADDITIONAL NICETIES AS CASSIA BARK, CORIANDER SEED, ANGELICA ROOT, AND ORRIS ROOT. THE PEEL OF CERTAIN CITRUS FRUITS WILL CERTAINLY BE THERE, NOT TO MENTION A FEW OTHER INSPIRATIONAL HERBS THAT ARE SECRET ONLY TO THE DISTILLER. TO MARTIN MILLER'S MIND THERE ARE USUALLY FOUR MAIN THINGS TO WATCH FOR IN A GOOD GIN. THE FIRST TO CONSIDER IS THE 'BASE' SPIRIT FROM WHICH THE GIN IS MADE BY RE-DISTILLATION; THIS MUST BE GRAIN SPIRIT OF THE HIGHEST QUALITY AND CONSISTENCY. SECOND, COMES THE RECIPE; WHICH BY STRICT TRADITION IS ALWAYS VERY SECRET. IT'S USUALLY SAFEGUARDED BY A RULE WHICH, FOR MORE THAN A CENTURY, HAS PERMITTED ONLY THREE HUMAN BEINGS TO HAVE KNOWLEDGE OF IT AT ANY ONE TIME. THIRDLY, THE INGREDIENTS THEMSELVES. IN THE DARK STOREROOMS OF THE DISTILLERY WILL STAND BINS AND BINS OF THEM AND IN THEIR MIDST

YOU WILL SEE THERMOMETERS STICKING UP LIKE POKERS, EACH TO ENSURE THE CORRECT LEVELS OF TEMPERATURE AND HUMIDITY. HERE THERE WILL BE DARK PURPLE, PUCKERED JUNIPER BERRIES, HARVESTED FROM THE HILLS OF TUSCANY, INDIA OR MACEDONIA. ALONGSIDE THESE WILL BE FOUND TINY, BUFF COLOURED CORIANDER SEEDS. THEN BESIDE THEM YOU MIGHT DISCOVER DESICCATED ANGELICA ROOTS, THEIR STRINGY HUSKS AND FIBRES DUG UP IN THE FIELDS OF SAXONY OR NORTHERN FRANCE; IT'S ONLY THERE THAT THE SOIL AND CLIMATE BRING OUT THEIR PROPER PUNGENCY. IT SHOULD HAVE A STRONG AROMATIC ODOUR, EVEN GINNIER THAN THE JUNIPER ITSELF. OTHER INGREDIENTS OF A SECRET SORT MAY ALSO FIGURE IN THE BOUQUET'S INDIVIDUALITY DEPENDING ON THE GIN AND THE PARTICULARITIES OF THE DISTILLER. LAST, BUT NOT LEAST, THE EQUIPMENT, THE GRAND SALLE-DE-DISTILLERY, IN MARTIN MILLER'S CASE A SINGLE, THREE STORIES HIGH, BALLOON BELLIED, SAMOVARISH POT STILL NAMED ANGELA, BUT MORE OF HER LATER.

"Supplementing the list of main things there is the little item of knowing how. For mere apparatus doesn't automatically make good gin."
MARTIN MILLER

COMMON GIN DISTILLATION

MOST GINS ARE DISTILLED USING THREE POTS, ONE OF THESE COPPERY BROWN BABES IS MARKED HIGH FEINTS AND ANOTHER LOW FEINTS, MEANING 'HEADS' AND 'TAILS'. THESE STILLS ARE USED TO RE-TREAT THE STUFF THAT COMES OVER AT THE BEGINNING AND END OF THE DISTILLATION NEITHER OF WHICH IS UP TO THE QUALITY OF THE MIDDLE OR 'HEART'. THAT IS TO SAY, WHEN YOU START OPERATIONS YOU DIVERT THE ORIGINAL RESULTS INTO THE 'HEADS' STILL, THEN AS THE HEART APPROACHES YOU DIVERT TO YOUR MAINLINE, THEN AS QUALITY BEGINS TO TAPER OFF YOU SHUNT THINGS OFF INTO THE 'TAILS' DEPARTMENT. THESE ODDS AND ENDS, TOO CRUDE FOR POLITE SOCIETY, ARE REDISTILLED AND LICKED INTO SHAPE, SO AS TO BE ABLE TO JOIN THE PARTY LATER ON.
ON ITS WAY THROUGH THE MAIN POT, THE SPIRIT VAPOUR PASSES A 'BERRY TRAY' OR CARTERHEAD.
THIS TRAY CONTAINS THE BOTANICALS. AS THE SPIRIT VAPOURS PASS THROUGH THE CARTERHEAD THEY ARE INFUSED WITH, AND EXTRACT, THE FLAVOURS AND OILS THAT GIVE THE GIN ITS CHARACTER AND TASTE.

MARTIN MILLER'S ON THE OTHER HAND USES A SINGLE POT, ANGELA. (DISTILLERS HAVE A FONDNESS FOR NAMING THEIR STILLS). ANGELA WAS MADE BACK IN 1904 BY JOHN DORE AND SONS, AND IS UNIVERSALLY ACCEPTED AS ONE OF THE 'ROLLS ROYCE' OF GIN STILLS.

FOR MARTIN MILLER'S GIN THERE IS NO PARTY FOR THE HEADS AND TAILS, BOTH ARE DISCARDED.

THE CENTRAL PART OF THE DISTILLATION, THE HEART, AND ONLY THE HEART OF THE SPIRIT IS KEPT.

NOW, NEITHER MARTIN MILLER, OR ANGELA FOR THAT MATTER, HOLD WITH 'BERRY TRAYS' OR CARTERHEADS.

MR. MILLER BRINGS HIS PHILOSOPHY OF TEA MAKING TO HIS GIN. NEVER A TEA BAG, ALWAYS REAL LOOSE TEA, AND LASHINGS OF BOILING WATER. FOR HIM THE TRADITIONAL, OLD FASHIONED METHOD WHERE THE BOTANICALS ARE CAREFULLY MEASURED, WEIGHED, THEN GENTLY STEEPED OVERNIGHT IN SPIRIT AND HOT WATER IS PREFERRED. IT MAY BE MESSY, IT MAY BE LABOUR INTENSIVE, BUT HE HOLDS THAT GENTLE MACERATION OVER AN EXTENDED PERIOD IS A FAR SUPERIOR TECHNIQUE FOR EXTRACTING EVERY NUANCE OF THE ESSENTIAL OILS AND FLAVOURS NECESSARY TO PRODUCE A SUPER PREMIUM GIN. EVEN IF, AS HE WOULD PUT IT, TO KEEP MATTERS UNDER CONTROL REQUIRES "ARTFUL FIGURING AND JUGGLING."

BUT CAN THE TRADITIONS OF GIN MAKING AND GIN DISTILLATION BE IMPROVED ON? WELL, MARTIN MILLER HAS ONE MORE TRICK UP HIS SLEEVE. IN ALL MARTIN MILLER'S GIN THE DRIED PEELS OF THE CITRUS FRUITS ARE DISTILLED SEPARATELY, AWAY FROM THE MORE GROUNDED, EARTHY, BOTANICALS SUCH AS JUNIPER.

SIMILAR TO TECHNIQUES USED IN HAUTE CUISINE MARTIN MILLER BELIEVES THIS SEPARATE DISTILLATION OR 'COOKING' OF THE INGREDIENTS CREATES A MORE BALANCED GIN WITH BRIGHTER CITRUS NOTES, WHEN COMPARED TO 'STEWING', OR DISTILLING EVERYTHING TOGETHER.

SETTING OUT TO CREATE HIS GIN, MARTIN MILLER AIMED TO MAKE A "FRESH SOFT GIN UNLIKE ANY OTHER"; A GIN WITH EXTREME CLARITY OF TASTE, WHERE THE REFRESHING QUALITY OF THE CITRUS FRUITS COULD COEXIST IN HARMONY WITH THE HEADIER JUNIPER BERRY. THIS IS MR. MILLER'S FAMOUS TWIST ON TRADITION.

"Of course I respect tradition, but it exists to be subverted"
MARTIN MILLER

THE STORY OF MARTIN MILLER'S GIN

ICELAND CHILLED

THE STORY OF MARTIN MILLER'S GIN

Nykur is the Icelandic water spirit. He appears usually in the form of a fine dapple-grey horse.
He may be distinguished from ordinary horses by the circumstance of his hooves being reversed.

"I wouldn't bet much on him for the Derby!"
MARTIN MILLER

THE STORY OF MARTIN MILLER'S GIN

LAND OF FIRE AND ICE

POLLUTION FREE, AND WITH ITS CHILLY NAME, ICELAND IS IN GEOLOGICAL TERMS A BIT OF A BABE. IT'S BEEN ONLY 20 MILLION YEARS SINCE THE NORTHERN ATLANTIC CAST UP THIS SPARSELY POPULATED, REMOTE AND BEAUTIFUL LAND. OFTEN CALLED THE 'LAND OF FIRE AND ICE', IT'S A TURBULENT AND CONTRADICTORY COUNTRY THAT CERTAINLY LIVES UP TO ITS NAME.

TURBULENT FOR SURE, HERE NATURE AND GEOLOGY CAN, AT A MOMENT'S NOTICE, OFFER SOME VERY NASTY SURPRISES - ICELAND IS AFTER ALL ONE OF THE WORLD'S MOST VOLCANICALLY ACTIVE HOT SPOTS AND BEING THERE IT IS EASY TO IMAGINE THE EARTH OPENING UP, SWALLOWING YOU, AND LEAVING NO TRACE WHATSOEVER. CONTRADICTORY TOO, IN THAT WHILE ONLY THE SIZE OF KENTUCKY, AND WITH A POPULATION OF JUST OVER 300,000, ICELAND IS, AT ONCE, ONE OF THE MOST SPARSELY POPULATED COUNTRIES IN THE WORLD, YET HAS ONE OF THE MOST DEVELOPED SOCIETIES. HOWEVER, UNTIL THE MIDDLE OF THE 20TH CENTURY ICELAND WAS ALSO ONE OF EUROPE'S POOREST COUNTRIES.

NOWADAYS, ICELAND IS A TECHNOLOGICALLY ADVANCED SOCIETY, 95% OF ADULTS OWN COMPUTERS. ADULT LITERACY IS 100%, AND MORE BOOKS PER CAPITA ARE WRITTEN AND PUBLISHED IN ICELAND THAN IN ANY OTHER NATION ON EARTH.

SO, ICELANDERS ARE LITERATE, TECHNICALLY ADVANCED AND SOCIALLY WELL BALANCED. IS THAT THE WHOLE STORY?

WELL NO; YOU DON'T HAVE TO LOOK FAR TO SEE EVEN MORE CONTRADICTORY FORCES AT WORK. BENEATH THIS URBANE, COOL SURFACE GLOSS, LIES A DEEPER, MORE PRIMITIVE BELIEF SYSTEM.

ICELAND, WITH ITS LONG DARK WINTERS AND SURREAL LAVA FORMATIONS, IS A HOTBED OF MYTHS AND LEGENDS THAT DATE BACK TO THE DAYS OF THE SAGAS AND THE VIKINGS. ICELANDERS STILL CLAIM THAT ONE IN EVERY 500 INHABITANTS OF ICELAND ARE EITHER ELVES OR TROLLS. TO THIS DAY, BELIEF IN ELVES OR THE HIDDEN PEOPLE CAN STILL HAVE BOTH SUBTLE AND, IN SOME CASES, QUITE OVERT INFLUENCES ON DAY TO DAY LIFE IN MODERN ICELAND.

"Although Iceland is miles from anywhere it's also halfway to most places as it is mid Atlantic.
So for Martin Miller's, bottling in Iceland using Iceland's carbon free energy and pure water
makes a lot of sense as so much of my gin goes to the United States."
MARTIN MILLER

THE STORY OF MARTIN MILLER'S GIN

ARCTIC CLARITY

ICELANDER'S ENJOY VERY CORDIAL RELATIONS WITH THEIR NEIGHBOURS FROM THE OTHER WORLD - THE HIDDEN PEOPLE. ICELANDERS BELIEVE THAT ELVES ARE THE CHILDREN THAT EVE HADN'T FINISHED WASHING WHEN GOD CAME TO VISIT. BECAUSE THEY WEREN'T FIT TO BE SEEN, SHE HAD NO CHOICE BUT TO HIDE THEM.

HENCE THEY ARE 'THE HIDDEN PEOPLE'. ELVES ARE TREATED WITH GREAT RESPECT. THE ROCKS, HILLS AND STREAMS IN WHICH THEY LIVE, ARE DILIGENTLY PRESERVED. ROADS ARE DIVERTED, ONE ROAD IN REYKJAVIK IS EVEN NAMED 'ELF HILL ROAD'. ON GRUNDARFJÖRDUR'S MAIN STREET, A ROCK STANDS BETWEEN HOUSES NUMBER 82 AND 86 - ELVES LIVE AT NUMBER 84.

"THE SECRET'S IN THE WATER"

BORGANES IS SITUATED AT THE HEAD OF A STUNNINGLY BEAUTIFUL FJORD ON ICELAND'S REMOTE WEST COAST. IT'S A TEN-DAY JOURNEY FOR MARTIN MILLER'S FROM IMMINGHAM, ON THE EAST COAST OF ENGLAND, ACROSS THE STORMY SEAS OF THE NORTH ATLANTIC TO THIS REMOTE VILLAGE; BUT IT'S WORTH IT.

ON AN ISLAND ALREADY FAMOUS FOR ITS SENSE OF MAGIC AND ATMOSPHERE, THIS IS A TRULY MAGICAL PLACE. BEHIND THE VILLAGE TO THE NORTH, STEEP AND FORBIDDING RISE THE 'RIDGES OF HELL' KNOWN AS HELGRINDUR TO THE ICELANDERS. BEYOND THAT, CAPPED WITH SNOW, CAN BE SEEN THE VOLCANIC CALDERA OF SNÆFELLSJÖKUL, JULES VERNE'S LEGENDARY GATEWAY TO THE CENTRE OF THE EARTH.

IT'S HERE WE BRING THE MARTIN MILLER'S SPIRIT FOR ITS ICELANDIC 'MARRIAGE'. IT'S HERE THAT THE ART OF THE BLENDER TAKES PLACE, WHERE REAL MAGIC IS WROUGHT. SPARKLING BRIGHT, PURE AND UNPOLLUTED WE DRAW WATER FROM OUR OWN SPRING. THIS IS WATER LIKE NO OTHER, ICY COLD AND ALIVE.

IT EMERGES INTO DAYLIGHT FOR THE FIRST TIME IN MAYBE 800 YEARS, RISING FROM THE DEPTHS OF THE BASALT MOUNTAINS THAT FRAME THE SKYLINE OF THIS SLEEPY VILLAGE.

SO, SPIRIT INTO SPIRIT, FOR ICELANDER'S TRULY BELIEVE THEIR WATER TO BE A LIVING ENTITY, MARTIN MILLER'S IS DELICATELY BLENDED WITH PURE ICELANDIC SPRING WATER CREATING A MARRIAGE OF RARE SOFTNESS, CLARITY OF TASTE AND APPEARANCE -

- IT IS SIMPLY BOTTLED MAGIC.

"Icelandic water really does have this magical quality. It's as if the surface is somehow elastic. In some way it seems to retain the volatiles and aromatics, holding onto them only to release them in a progressive and ordered way, giving my gin its distinctive gentleness."

MARTIN MILLER

*"I'm not influenced by fashion. It's too transient.
I'm more interested in timelessness. Then again, something
doesn't need to be ancient or traditional to be a classic."*

MARTIN MILLER

GIN. BY JUNIPER!

"Some things are not what they appear to be.
Take the Juniper berry. It isn't a berry at all,
in fact it is a cone with unusually fleshy scales
that just give it the appearance of a berry."
MARTIN MILLER

GIN. BY JUNIPER!

ELIXIRS AND POTIONS

THE OIL OF THE JUNIPER BERRY IS ONE OF THE EARLIEST ESSENTIAL OILS EXTRACTED BY MAN. EVIDENCE OF ITS EXTRACTION AND USE DATES BACK TO PREHISTORIC TIMES. JUNIPER HAS BEEN USED BY MANY CULTURES OVER THE CENTURIES. ITS OIL IS REPORTED TO HAVE BEEN USED BY THE EGYPTIANS DURING BURIAL CEREMONIES AND IN THEIR COSMETICS AND PERFUMES. THE ANCIENT GREEKS RECORD USING JUNIPER BERRIES AS A MEDICINE, PARTICULARLY AS A REMEDY FOR RHEUMATISM AND ARTHRITIS, AS WELL AS A DIURETIC AND APPETITE STIMULANT. IN MEDIEVAL EUROPE IT WAS USED TO FIGHT DEADLY INFECTIONS LIKE TYPHOID AND CHOLERA, WITH DECIDEDLY MIXED RESULTS.

THE BUSINESS OF COMBINING LIQUOR AND PLANT LIFE GOES BACK TO THE DAWN OF DISTILLING.

IN PRIMITIVE DAYS, ALCOHOLIC DRINKS WERE SO BRUTAL AND BELCHFUL, THAT ANYTHING, BARK, BERRY OR ROOT, WAS GRABBED AT TO MAKE THEM MORE PALATABLE.

IN SOME CULTURES GINGER PROVED HELPFUL, PRESAGING GINGER BEER. EVEN PEPPER WAS USED.

BUT JUNIPER PROVED THE PERENNIAL FAVOURITE.

THE HISTORY OF GIN AND THE JUNIPER BERRY ARE INEXTRICABLY LINKED, BUT WHERE AND WHO IT WAS THAT MADE THAT FIRST LEAP FROM MEDICINE TO MARTINI IS A SUBJECT OF CLAIM AND COUNTER CLAIM. ARCHEOLOGISTS HAVE CERTAINLY DISCOVERED THAT OUR EUROPEAN ANCESTORS USED JUNIPER TO FLAVOUR THE BEER THEY DRANK. ITALIAN MONKS WERE USING THEIR OWN PLENTIFUL SUPPLIES OF JUNIPER TO MAKE MEDICINAL POTIONS AND ELIXIRS IN THE 11TH CENTURY. HOWEVER, FRANCE AND THE LOWLANDS FIGURE MORE PROMINENTLY AS THE LIKELY BIRTHPLACE OF GIN AS A SOCIAL DRINK RATHER THAN A MEDICINE AND BY THE TURN OF THE 16TH CENTURY THE DISTILLATION OF SPIRITS, WHETHER FROM GRAIN OR GRAPE WAS COMMONPLACE. THE RESULTANT SPIRIT, KNOWN AS BRANDEWIJN, LITERALLY 'BURNT WINE' USUALLY TASTED, AS THE NAME SUGGESTS, BURNT AND BITTER.

TO EASE THE PAIN, INVENTIVE SOULS BENT THEIR MINDS TO CREATING WAYS IN WHICH THE INTOXICATING NATURE OF THIS LIQUOR COULD BE MADE MORE PALATABLE.

THE USUAL SUSPECT WAS, MORE OFTEN THAN NOT, JUNIPER.

" One of my favourite nicknames for gin is the 18th century one, Tityre.
So called, because it made persons merry, laugh, and titter.
Certainly the only depressing thing about my gin is the price!"
MARTIN MILLER

GIN. BY JUNIPER!

OF PROFESSORS AND BASTARDS

THE FRENCH CLAIM THEY WERE THE FIRST TO PUT JUNIPER TO GOOD USE AS A PALLIATIVE, EASING THE PAIN INVOLVED IN THE CONSUMPTION OF SPIRITS DISTILLED DURING THIS EARLY PERIOD, THOUGH THE DUTCH MAY WELL DISPUTE THE FACT.

PLEADING THE CASE FOR THE FRENCH IS ONE ANTOINE DE BOURBON, COUNT DE MORET, THE RESULT OF A BRIEF AFFAIR BETWEEN KING HENRY OF NAVARRE AND THE COMTESSE DE MORET. HE WAS BORN A BASTARD IN 1607, BUT LATER IN LIFE HIS BIRTH WAS LEGITIMIZED AND HIS FATHER GRANTED HIM THE ABBÉ DE ST ETIENNE. LIKE ALL ECCLESIASTICAL GENTLEMEN OF THE PERIOD HIS MIND SOON STRAYED TO THINGS ALCOHOLIC, AND IN HIS SHORT LIFE HE PERFECTED SOMETHING HE CALLED JUNIPER WINE, PROBABLY USING A BASE SPIRIT DISTILLED FROM THE GRAPE. WHETHER CLAIMING 'SIMULTANEOUS CREATION' OR JUST PLAIN CHEATING, AROUND THE SAME TIME, AND IN THE NOBLE CAUSE OF MEDICAL RESEARCH (THIS BEING THE PROTESTANT LOWLANDS), THE FAMOUS DUTCH PROFESSOR, FRANCISCUS DE LA BOE, PERHAPS BETTER KNOWN AS FRANZ SYLVIUS, DISCOVERED WHAT THE AROMATIC JUNIPER BERRY COULD DO FOR A SLUG OF RAW ALCOHOL. JUNIPER COMBINED ALTOGETHER MORE SUCCESSFULLY WITH THE GRAINY, MALTY FLAVOUR OF THEIR DISTILLED SPIRITS, WHICH WERE GENERALLY DERIVED FROM WHEAT AND BARLEY. NAMING IT GENIÈVRE IN HONOUR OF THE BERRY, PROFESSOR SYLVIUS IS NOW THE NAME MOST QUOTED AS THE INVENTOR AND FATHER OF GIN. IT'S ALTOGETHER MORE LIKELY THAT MANY SOULS WERE EXPERIMENTING WITH DISTILLATES AND FLAVOURINGS AT THE TIME, SO PERHAPS IT IS MORE APPROPRIATE TO LABEL HIM AS ONE OF THE WORLD'S FIRST GREAT BRAND BUILDERS (OR MAYBE HE JUST HIRED A BETTER P.R.).

TODAY, JUNIPER IS STILL THE SINGLE INGREDIENT THAT DEFINES GIN. THE QUALITY OF THE BERRY AND THE WAY IN WHICH ITS OILS ARE EXTRACTED ALL PLAY A PART IN CREATING THE CHARACTER OF FINE GINS. THAT IS WHY MARTIN MILLER SOURCES HIS JUNIPER FROM WHEREVER THE BEST BERRIES ARE TO BE FOUND, WHETHER THAT IS TUSCANY, MACEDONIA, OR AS FAR AWAY AS INDIA, IS IRRELEVANT. HE DEMANDS ONLY THE FINEST QUALITY JUNIPER, WITH THE HIGHEST OIL AND FLAVOUR CONTENT.

"Most people don't realise that Juniper can grow in many regions of the world, but I use only the best berries for Martin Miller's. These are traditionally found in Tuscany and Macedonia. Increasingly though, with climate change, I'm finding that India is proving an invaluable source, producing plump oil rich berries."
MARTIN MILLER

THE STORY OF MARTIN MILLER'S GIN

"Gin isn't a boring grain neutral spirit like vodka.
Gin looks out on the world.
It is the spirit of adventure."
MARTIN MILLER

SILK ROADS AND SPICE ROUTES

THE STORY OF MARTIN MILLER'S GIN

*"Gin is the most seductive of drinks. It's not only history
in a glass, it's romance and adventure too."*
MARTIN MILLER

THE SPICE OF LIFE

FORTUNES WON AND LOST, KINGS AND EMPERORS SEDUCED, NATIONS SUBJUGATED, ALL IN THE NAME OF SPICE.

SPICES FLATTER OUR SENSES AND CAST SPELLS OVER OUR IMAGINATION. SPICES HAVE BEEN INSTRUMENTAL IN SOME OF HUMANITY'S GREATEST ADVENTURES AND, TO THIS DAY, INVITE US TO EXPLORE - EVEN IF WE NEVER TRAVEL FURTHER THAN THE NEAREST BAR. TRY IT, PLACE YOUR NOSE INTO A MARTIN MILLER'S GIN AND TONIC AND FEEL YOURSELF ENERGISED AND REMINDED OF JOURNEYS TO EXOTIC PLACES.

BEFORE THE DISCOVERY OF THE SEA ROUTE TO INDIA THE SILK ROAD LINKED THE ORIENT AND THE WEST, STRETCHING FROM THE MEDITERRANEAN TO CHINA. ALONG THIS ROAD TRAVELLED MARCO POLO, BEFORE HIM THE ROMANS, AND BEFORE THEM, ALEXANDER THE GREAT. BY THE 15TH CENTURY THIS ROUTE HAD BECOME TOO HAZARDOUS DUE TO TRIBAL RAIDERS; SO AT ITS FAR EASTERN END THE CHINESE COLLECTED CLOVES AND NUTMEG FROM THE EAST INDIES AND DELIVERED THEM TO THE MALAYSIAN PORT OF MALACCA. HERE MUSLIM

MERCHANTS FROM INDIA, MALAYA OR ARABIA TRANSPORTED THE GOODS ACROSS THE BAY OF BENGAL TO INDIA WHERE CINNAMON FROM CEYLON WAS ADDED TO THE CARGO TO BE SOLD ON IN THE SPICE PORTS OF KOLKATA, COCHIN AND GOA.

AS ARABS CONTROLLED THE INDIAN OCEAN, DHOWS SAILED FROM INDIA TO PERSIA, ARABIA, AND ONWARD TO EAST AFRICA, PICKING UP CARGOES OF CASSIA BARK AND EVERY MANNER OF EXOTIC SPICES ALONG THE WAY. FROM ZANZIBAR THE NOW FULLY LADEN DHOWS MADE THEIR WAY UP THE RED SEA PAST ADEN AND ON TO THE PORT OF BAB-EL-MANDEB. FROM HERE THE PRECIOUS CARGO WAS TRANSFERRED TO EGYPTIAN VESSELS FOR THE JOURNEY THROUGH THE NILE VALLEY TO CAIRO.

IN CAIRO THE SPOILS WERE DIVIDED AND TAKEN BY RIVER BOAT AND CAMEL CARAVAN TO ALEPPO, DAMASCUS OR CONSTANTI-NOPLE. FROM THESE PORTS TRANSPORT COULD BE ARRANGED ON ITALIAN SHIPS BOUND FOR VENICE AND GENOA.

HERE, WEALTHY ITALIAN MERCHANTS WOULD SEND THEM TO GRACE THE DINING TABLES OF GERMANY, AND FRANCE; OR IN ANNUAL CONVOYS OF ITALIAN GALLEYS THROUGH THE STRAITS OF GIBRALTER TO ENGLAND, THE NORTH AND LOW COUNTRIES.

"Such was the wealth of these Italian merchants, and the profit that they made from the spice trade, it is said that they could afford to lose 4 out of every 5 shipments of goods to storms or pirates and still make a healthy profit."

THE SPICE OF LIFE

THE RACE FOR CONTROL OF SPICES WAS WELL AND
TRULY ON; THE PORTUGUESE, SPANISH, DUTCH, FRENCH
AND ENGLISH WERE SOON ALL IN ON THE ACTION,
SETTING UP FACTORIES, FORTS AND EVENTUALLY
COLONIES ALL ACROSS THE INDIAN OCEAN IN ORDER TO
PROTECT THEIR CONTROL OVER THE PRODUCTION OF
VARIOUS SPICES.

IN 1708 THE EAST INDIA COMPANY WAS FORMED BY A
MERGER OF TWO RIVAL COMPANIES TO TRADE WITH THE
"INDIES." IT WAS TO BECOME THE STRONGEST EUROPEAN
POWER ON THE COAST OF INDIA, ABLE TO ENFORCE ITS
WILL ON THE NATIVE RULERS. BY THE MIDDLE OF THE
18TH CENTURY, OVER TWO THIRDS OF THAT VAST
SUB-CONTINENT WAS RULED BY THE COMPANY.

AS A RESULT THERE WERE LARGE NUMBERS OF BRITISH
TROOPS AND EX-PATRIOT CIVILIANS IN COLONIAL INDIA.
MALARIA WAS A PROBLEM, AND THE ONLY KNOWN
PREVENTATIVE WAS TO DRINK MASSIVE AMOUNTS OF
QUININE. QUININE DRUNK NEAT IS EXTREMELY BITTER,
SO A VARIETY OF CONCOCTIONS WERE DREAMT UP TO
MAKE THE REQUIRED DOSE TASTE BETTER.

ONE SOLUTION WAS TO ADD A BIT OF GIN TO THE
MEDICINE, AND SO THE GIN AND TONIC WAS BORN.
NOW, VAST NUMBERS OF EX-PATRIOT BRITISH DRINKING
VAST AMOUNTS OF GIN CREATED A PROBLEM: THERE
SIMPLY WASN'T ENOUGH GIN IN INDIA. HOWEVER, LOCAL
ENTREPRENEURS WHO BUILT THEIR OWN GIN STILLS
RAPIDLY FILLED THE VACUUM.

ONE PROBLEM THEY ENCOUNTERED WAS THAT THE
ENGLISH AND DUTCH RECIPES OF THE TIME CONTAINED
BOTANICALS THAT WERE EXPENSIVE TO IMPORT INTO
INDIA. THE DISTILLERIES IMPROVISED USING BOTANICALS
AND AROMATICS THAT WERE READY TO HAND, AND A NEW
STYLE OF GIN WAS BORN.

THESE GINS GAVE LESS EMPHASIS TO JUNIPER. THEY HAD
A SOFTER LESS 'PINEY' NOSE AND TENDED TO HAVE A
HIGHER ALCOHOLIC STRENGTH. THE EXOTIC BOTANICAL
INFUSIONS IN INDIAN STYLE GINS WERE SPICY AND
INTRIGUING IN A WAY THAT OTHER GINS WERE NOT AND
PROVED EXTREMELY POPULAR. TODAY MARTIN MILLER
HAS DEVELOPED HIS WESTBOURNE STRENGTH GIN AS
THE FINEST AVAILABLE EXPRESSION OF THIS STYLE OF GIN.

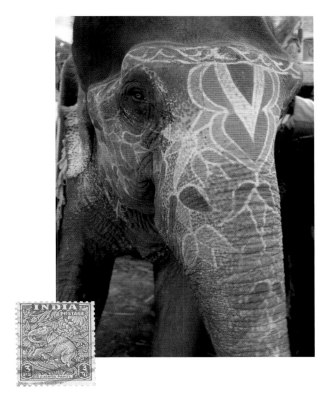

*"Every time I get the shivers I'm convinced it's the onset of Malaria.
The only solution to my chronic hypochondria is a refreshing
Martin Miller's and tonic!"*
MARTIN MILLER

THE STORY OF MARTIN MILLER'S GIN

MANY VARIETIES OF ORANGES ARE USED FOR THEIR
ESSENTIAL OIL, BUT IT IS THE BITTER, DRIED RIND OF THE
SEVILLE ORANGE, FIRST BOUGHT TO SPAIN BY THE MOORS,
THAT IS USED IN THE MAKING OF MARTIN MILLER'S GIN.
IT IS, AFTER JUNIPER, THE MOST IMPORTANT BOTANICAL
IN THE MAKE UP OF GIN. THE DRIED OUTER RIND IS USED
BECAUSE ITS BITTERNESS IS MOST DESIRABLE AS IT ADDS
AN AROMATIC, BRIGHT AND REFRESHING DIMENSION TO
THE PALATE.

THIS 'REFRESHING BRIGHTNESS' IS VERY MUCH THE
SIGNATURE OF BOTH TYPES OF MARTIN MILLER'S GINS.
THE DELICATE BALANCE OF CITRUS AND JUNIPER,
WHERE NEITHER DOMINATES, IS ACHIEVED BY THE
INNOVATIVE SEPARATE DISTILLATION OF THE CITRUS
ELEMENTS WHICH ALSO INCLUDES SOME DRIED LEMON
AND LIME RIND. THIS DISTILLATE IS THEN 'MARRIED', TO
THE EARTHIER JUNIPER BASED DISTILLATE LATER ON IN A
SEPARATE PROCESS.

WHEN HE SET OUT TO CREATE HIS GIN, MARTIN MILLER'S
AIM WAS TO CREATE "A CLASSIC GIN LIKE NO OTHER".
THIS IS MARTIN MILLER'S FAMOUS 'TWIST ON TRADITION'.

MANY GINS LAY CLAIM TO A CAST OF THOUSANDS WHEN LISTING THEIR BOTANICALS. MARTIN MILLER, HOWEVER, BELIEVES THAT AN EPIC CAST DOES NOT NECESSARILY PRODUCE AN EPIC GIN.

HE FEELS NO NEED FOR EXOTIC AND OBSCURE INGREDIENTS OR FOR A CHORUS OF BOTANICALS THAT SERVE ONLY TO DROWN OUT THE SHOW'S STAR.

RATHER, MARTIN MILLER'S GIN IS, AND ALWAYS HAS BEEN, A DRY GIN IN THE CLASSIC SENSE, WITH A WELL CHOSEN, BALANCED CAST OF BOTANICALS. TOP BILLING OF COURSE IS GIVEN TO JUNIPER THEN, IN SUPPORT, CORIANDER, ANGELICA, LIME PEEL, LIQUORICE ROOT, CASSIA BARK AND FLORENTINE IRIS. LIKE A WELL REHEARSED TROUPE THEY GO ABOUT THEIR BUSINESS, DOING WHAT THEY HAVE ALWAYS DONE, AND DOING IT WELL. CORIANDER GIVES THE DISTINCTIVE AROMAS OF GINGER, SAGE AND LEMON; WHILE ANGELICA IMPARTS ITS WOODY DRYNESS. LIQUORICE AND CASSIA ROOT ADD SWEETNESS AND SPICY AROMAS IN EQUAL MEASURE AND LIME PEEL ADDS EXTRA FRESHNESS. FINALLY, UNDERPINNING AND BINDING IT ALL TOGETHER, IS THE AROMATIC AND FLORAL FLORENTINE IRIS.

CORIANDER: *ALSO COMMONLY CALLED CILANTRO CORIANDER SEEDS ARE TYPICALLY USED IN CONJUNCTION WITH ORANGE PEEL TO ADD A SULTRY CITRUS CHARACTER*

ANGELICA: *SOMETIMES USED IN THE MAKING OF ABSINTHE, ANGELICA GROWS WILD IN FINLAND AND ICELAND. IT'S ALSO KNOWN AS 'HOLY GHOST ROOT'. IT'S THOUGHT TO BE A POWERFUL GUARDIAN AND HEALER.*

LIME PEEL: *RICH IN ESSENTIAL OILS LIME PEEL DISTILLED WITH THE EARTHIER BOTANICALS CREATES A 'CITRUS BRIDGE' BETWEEN THEM AND THE SEPARATELY DISTILLED BITTER ORANGE AND LEMON, CREATING AN UNMATCHED BRILLIANCE TO THE CITRUS FLAVOUR OF MARTIN MILLER'S*

LIQUORICE ROOT: *THE WORD 'LIQUORICE' IS DERIVED FROM THE ANCIENT GREEK WORDS FOR 'SWEET ROOT'. IT'S ACTIVE PRINCIPLE IS GLYCYRRHIZIN, A SWEETENER MORE THAN 50 TIMES AS SWEET AS SUCROSE.*

CASSIA BARK: *SIMILAR IN MANY RESPECTS TO CINNAMON BUT STRONGER STILL AND MORE AROMATIC; IN CHINESE MEDICINE IT IS USED TO TREAT IMPOTENCE AND FRIGIDITY.*

FLORENTINE IRIS: *PERHAPS THE LEADING ACTOR IN THE SUPPORTING CAST. THE FLORAL AND AROMATIC FLORENTINE IRIS (SEE BELOW) BINDS AND UNITES THE VOLATILITY OF THE OTHER TEAM MEMBERS AND ENSURES HARMONIOUS, ORDERLY AND SUBTLE RELEASE OF FLAVOUR.*

"To my mind style for the sake of style runs contrary to my pursuit of perfection. It will always lead to compromise. Perfection can only be achieved through attention to detail. That's our secret ingredient, our obsessive attention to detail"
MARTIN MILLER

THE STORY OF MARTIN MILLER'S GIN

GIN.

THE DUTCH INVENTED IT,

THE ENGLISH REFINED IT,

AND THE YANKS GLAMOURISED IT.

NOW MARTIN MILLER'S HAS PERFECTED IT.

THE STORY OF MARTIN MILLER'S GIN

GIN LANE DENIED

GIN. THE DUTCH INVENTED IT, THE ENGLISH
REFINED IT, AND THE YANKS GLAMOURISED IT.
GIN HAS CERTAINLY COME A LONG WAY SINCE
THE DAYS WHEN ENGLISH GIN MILLS ADVERTISED
"DRUNK FOR A PENNY, DEAD DRUNK FOR
TUPPENCE, CLEAN STRAW FOR NOTHING."
HOWEVER, THE GIN DRUNK THEN, KNOWN AS 'OLD
TOM', WAS SWEET AND BORE LITTLE OR NO
RESEMBLANCE TO THE DRIER, REFINED PRODUCTS
WE DRINK TODAY.
SO IT PUZZLES MARTIN MILLER THAT SO MANY GIN
BRANDS STILL DWELL ON THEIR 'HOGARTHIAN'
ROOTS IN GIN LANE AND ALL THE NEGATIVE
'BAGGAGE' THAT IT BRINGS. MARTIN MILLER DID NOT
START TO DISTIL HIS GIN UNTIL 1998, SO HE LAYS
NO CLAIM TO THAT PARTICULAR HERITAGE.
HE BELIEVES THAT GIN IS MORE TRUTHFULLY A
SPIRIT OF THE MODERN AGE, AND THAT GIN'S
STORY IS INEXTRICABLY LINKED WITH THE BIRTH
OF COCKTAILS, AND THE ALL-CONQUERING
MARTINI IN PARTICULAR.

*"I would take quality and improvement over heritage any day of the week.
When people ask me, "What heritage does your gin have?" I tell them,
"My gin goes all the way back to the dying days of the last century!"*
MARTIN MILLER

THE STORY OF MARTIN MILLER'S GIN

"RIDING THE GILDED JUGGERNAUT OF JAZZ AND GIN"

THE DRY GINS WE KNOW TODAY REALLY CAME OF AGE WITH THE BIRTH OF THE 20TH CENTURY. AROUND THAT TIME AMERICA'S GRAND HOTELS TOOK THE ENGLISH INSTITUTION OF FIVE-O-CLOCK TEA AND TRANSFORMED IT INTO THE 'COCKTAIL HOUR' IN FACT, EARLY SHAKERS WERE MODELLED ON TEAPOTS AND THESE 'SOIREES' WERE KNOWN AS 'TEAS' WELL INTO THE THIRTIES.

IN EARLIER TIMES, COCKTAILS, EVEN THE MARTINI WERE SWEET AFFAIRS BUT THIS NEW TIME SLOT DEMANDED A DRIER, APPETITE STIMULANT. THE NEW DRIER, GIN MARTINIS FITTED THE BILL PERFECTLY.

THEN, ON THE STROKE OF MIDNIGHT, JANUARY 16TH,1920, THE WHOLE OF AMERICA WENT DRIER STILL.

WITH THE ARRIVAL OF PROHIBITION CIRCUMSTANCE DEMANDED THAT HIGH SOCIETY RUB SHOULDERS WITH GANGSTERS IN SPEAKEASIES AND 'BLIND PIGS'. HERE THEY WERE EXPOSED TO THE NEW, EXCITING AND DANGEROUS WORLD OF GIN, 'JANES' AND JAZZ.

IT WAS PROHIBITION THAT GAVE GIN ATTITUDE, AND FOR SOME TO DRINK GIN WAS TO DEFEND THE VALUES OF MODERN CIVILISATION.

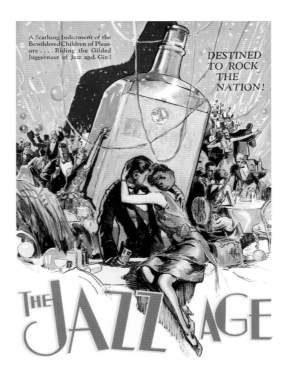

"Martinis are like breasts, one isn't enough, and three is too many."
HERB CAEN

THE STORY OF MARTIN MILLER'S GIN

GIN AND VERMOUTH, A MARRIAGE OF EQUALS

GIN'S URBANITY SURVIVED PROHIBITION AS DID ITS
ASSOCIATION WITH MORE OPEN ATTITUDES IN GENERAL.
WHEN THE VOLSTEAD ACT WAS REPEALED AND GIN WAS
ONCE AGAIN OPENLY ADVERTISED, IT USUALLY FEATURED
ATTRACTIVE, UNATTACHED COUPLES SIPPING GIN IN
ROMANTIC SETTINGS. MOVIES OF THE PERIOD ALSO
CARRIED OVER THIS ETHOS OF SEXY AND EQUAL
COMPANIONSHIP BETWEEN MEN AND WOMEN. THIS FREE
AND EASY ATTITUDE WAS EXEMPLIFIED BY DOROTHY PARKER,
WHOSE GROUP OF WRITERS MET WEEKLY FOR COCKTAILS
AND CONVERSATION AROUND THE FAMOUS ROUND TABLE
IN NEW YORK'S ALGONQUIN HOTEL; SHE WROTE:

> *I love to drink martinis*
> *Two at the very most*
> *Three I'm under the table*
> *Four I'm under the host"*

BETWEEN THE WARS COCKTAILS CAME TO SYMBOLISE
AMERICA'S NEW FOUND SELF CONFIDENCE.
TRANSATLANTIC TRAVEL ON THE LUXURIOUS CUNARD
LINERS ENCOURAGED THE EXPORT OF COCKTAILS TO THE
SWANKIEST TABLES OF EUROPE. IT WAS GIN THAT PUT

SOPHISTICATED GLOSS ON THE FEIGNED 'ENNUI' OF
LONDON'S 'BRIGHT YOUNG THINGS', AND, BY THE LATE
'30'S, GIN'S MODERN, INTERCONTINENTAL CREDENTIALS
COULD FIND NO HIGHER AUTHORITY THAN WHEN A
RECENTLY ABDICATED ENGLISH KING CELEBRATED HIS
NEW AMERICAN BRIDE BY CHRISTENING A GIN
COCKTAIL THE 'WALLIS BLUE*' IN HONOUR OF HER EYES.
GIN WAS WELL AND TRULY OUT OF THE 'ALLEY'.

A RECIPE FOR THE WALLIS BLUE CAN BE FOUND AT THE BACK OF THIS BOOK

"Let's slip out of these wet clothes and into a dry Martini."
ROBERT BENCHLEY

SEE THROUGHS AND SILVER BULLETS

PERFECTED BETWEEN THE WARS, THE MODERN GIN MARTINI RECIPE LACKED ONLY ONE THING TO ENABLE IT TO FULFIL ITS AESTHETIC DESTINY. NEW PROCESSES OF FILTRATION AND STABILISATION HAD ALL BUT ELIMINATED THE YELLOWISH TINT PRESENT IN VERMOUTH.

SO BY THE TIME THAT ROOSEVELT MIXED MARTINIS FOR CHURCHILL AND STALIN IN TEHRAN THE GIN MARTINI HAD BECOME AN AMERICAN ICON, AT ONCE CLEAR AND CIVILISED, YET POTENT; EXACTLY THE FACE THAT AMERICA WISHED TO SHOW THE WORLD.

THE GIN MARTINI HAD BECOME AMERICA'S STATE COCKTAIL, MIXED IN THE WHITE HOUSE, BY THE PRESIDENT HIMSELF. NICKNAMED 'THE CHILDREN'S HOUR' F.D.R WOULD GATHER HIS STAFF IN THE AFTERNOON FOR MARTINIS, ACCOMPANIED BY WHAT HE CALLED 'UNCLE JOE'S BOUNTY' - COPIOUS AMOUNTS OF CAVIAR GIFTED BY STALIN.

BY THE MID FIFTIES THE GIN MARTINI, CLEAR, STRONG AND DRY HAD RETURNED TO BEING A MAN'S DRINK, AND, IN AN ERA OF COLD WAR AND WITCH HUNTS, A LAST BASTION OF STANDARDS IN A LESS THAN PERFECT WORLD. DEAN ACHESON, TRUMAN'S SECRETARY OF STATE REMARKED THAT HE "LIKED DRINKING SOMETHING TRANSPARENT AFTER ALL THE MURKY TRANSACTIONS OF STATECRAFT." THIS WAS ALSO THE ERA OF THE THREE MARTINI LUNCH. THE MARTINIS WERE SERVED ULTRA DRY, AND KNOWN AS 'SEE THROUGHS' OR 'SILVER BULLETS'. BUT THIS NEW, MALE CORPORATE CULTURE THAT THE MARTINI EMBODIED SAT UNEASILY WITH THE FREEWHEELING ATTITUDES OF THE SIXTIES. THE MARTINI HAD BECOME CONSERVATIVE AND SUBURBAN; RATHER THAN BEING AN ICON OF CIVILISATION AND TRUTH IT HAD COME TO REFLECT AMERICAN CYNICISM AND FALSEHOOD. THIS CHANGE IN MEANING OF THE MARTINI CERTAINLY CONTRIBUTED TO ITS TWO DECADES OF SLOW DECLINE THAT STARTED IN THE SEVENTIES AND RAN INTO THE NINETIES. IN DEFIANCE, THE MARTINI TURNED MACHO. THE EASY GOING SEXUAL EQUALITY OF CARY GRANT AND KATHLEEN HEPBURN WAS OUT, THE MARTINI BECAME EXCLUSIVELY MALE, ITS ACOLYTES, DEAN MARTIN, FRANK SINATRA AND THE RAT PACK; BUT FOR ALL ITS MACHO BLUSTER, THE MARTINI WAS UNDER SIEGE, AND THE ENEMY HAD STEALTH ON ITS SIDE. IT WAS COLOURLESS, FLAVOURLESS AND TASTELESS.

THE 'AMUSING ANTIQUE'

"THE PAST IS A FOREIGN COUNTRY; THEY DO THINGS DIFFERENTLY THERE"

LIKE MANY AMERICAN ICONS, THE MARTINI DIDN'T READILY SURVIVE THE '60's. IN HIS 1976 ELECTION CAMPAIGN JIMMY CARTER DENOUNCED THE 'THREE MARTINI LUNCH'. IT WAS A THINLY VEILED ATTACK ON CORPORATE AMERICA. HE WAS NOT RE-ELECTED. NONETHELESS, THE '70's WAS THE DECADE OF MINERAL WATER, WHITE WINE AND VODKA, AND BY 1976 VODKA HAD SURPASSED GIN TO BECOME THE MOST WIDELY CONSUMED SPIRIT IN THE U. S.

THE SWITCH TO VODKA HAD ALREADY RECEIVED A MASSIVE BOOST IN THE '60's WHEN, BY A STROKE OF PURE GENIUS A LEADING VODKA BRAND PERSUADED A CERTAIN ENGLISH SPY TO ORDER HIS MARTINIS MIXED WITH VODKA, NOT GIN. THE DIE WAS CAST. AS THE SPIRIT CHANGED, SO DID THE MARTINI. IT BECAME LESS ELITE; IT WAS DRUNK ON THE ROCKS IN A 'LOWBALL' GLASS AND VODKA WAS MORE LIKELY THAN GIN TO BE ITS BACKBONE. BY 1985 TIME MAGAZINE DECLARED THE MARTINI AN 'AMUSING ANTIQUE', AND IN 1993 THE THREE MARTINI LUNCH WAS CONSIGNED TO HISTORY BY CHANGES IN U.S. TAX LAWS.

IRONICALLY, IT WAS NOW THE TIDE TURNED. THE COLD WAR HAD BEEN WON AND THE BERLIN WALL WAS DOWN; PUNK AND GRUNGE CULTURE WAS ASCENDANT; YET WHILE THEIR PARENTS AND CORPORATE AMERICA SWIGGED FIZZY WATER AND VODKA, A 'YOUNGER SET' WERE PURSUING NEW IDEAS AND SEEKING OUT OLDER MORAL CERTAINTIES. THEY FOUND THEM IN A FOREIGN COUNTRY: THE PAST.

THE GLASS WAS THE FIRST TO RETURN, WITH ITS ICONIC, DECO STYLE SO EVOCATIVE OF THIRTIES HOLLYWOOD, CIGARS AND NIGHTCLUBS. THEN, IN THE NAME OF AUTHENTICITY, GIN REPLACED VODKA AND, IN AN IMAGE OF CRYSTALLINE PERFECTION THE MARTINI RESOLVED ITSELF. THE CIRCLE WAS COMPLETE.

ONCE AGAIN THE MARTINI MEANT SOMETHING; ONCE AGAIN IT WAS, COOL, URBANE, SMART AND SEXY.

"How can a Martini made with vodka be called a Martini?
That's like vegetarian meatballs! Practically a contradiction in terms.
If you really have to call it something call it a Vodkatini."
MARTIN MILLER

MARTINIS, SHAKEN AND STIRRED

MARTINI

60ML MARTIN MILLER'S WESTBOURNE STRENGTH GIN
5ML DRY VERMOUTH

METHOD: SHAKE OR STIR USING VERY COLD ICE,
STRAIN INTO CHILLED GLASS
GLASS: COCKTAIL/MARTINI
GARNISH: OLIVES OR TWIST OF LEMON PEEL

DELMONICO

50ML MARTIN MILLER'S GIN
25ML DRY VERMOUTH
DASH ORANGE BITTERS

METHOD: STIR DOWN WITH CUBED ICE,
STRAIN INTO CHILLED GLASS
GLASS: MARTINI
GARNISH: OLIVES

GIBSON

60ML MARTIN MILLER'S WESTBOURNE STRENGTH GIN
5ML DRY VERMOUTH

METHOD: SHAKE OR STIR USING VERY COLD ICE,
STRAIN INTO CHILLED GLASS
GLASS: COCKTAIL/MARTINI
GARNISH: SILVERSKIN ONIONS

SHAKEN OR STIRRED?

IN THIS INSTANCE, MARTIN MILLER LIKES TO QUOTE THE AMERICAN HISTORIAN AND
SOCIAL COMMENTATOR, BERNARD DE VOTO, "THIS PERFECT THING IS MADE OF GIN AND
VERMOUTH, THEY ARE SELF RELIANT LIQUORS, STABLE, AND STOUT OF HEART;
WE DO NOT HAVE TO TREAT THEM AS IF THEY WERE PLOVER'S EGGS." YOU DECIDE.

"You can no more keep a Martini in the refrigerator than you can keep a kiss there.
The proper union of gin and vermouth is . . . one of the happiest marriages on earth, and one of the shortest lived."
BERNARD DeVOTO

THE STORY OF MARTIN MILLER'S GIN

SOUTHSIDE

GLASS: HI-BALL
METHOD: BUILD AND SWIZZLE WITH
CRUSHED ICE IN A HI-BALL
GARNISH: MINT SPRIG

50ML MARTIN MILLER'S GIN
20ML LIME JUICE
20ML SIMPLE SYRUP
8 MINT LEAVES
SODA

ALEXANDER

GLASS: MARTINI
METHOD: SHAKE AND STRAIN
INTO A COCKTAIL GLASS
GARNISH: NUTMEG

40ML MARTIN MILLER'S GIN
20ML CRÈME DE CACAO BLANC
20MM CREAM

BLOODY MARY

GLASS: HI-BALL
METHOD: BUILD IN A LONG GLASS
WITH CUBED ICE
GARNISH: RED CHILLI OR CELERY STICK

50ML MARTIN MILLER'S GIN
120ML TOMATO JUICE
3 DASHES TABASCO
2 DASHES OF LEA & PERRINS
PINCH OF CELERY SALT
SALT AND PEPPER

GIMLET

GLASS: MARTINI
METHOD: SHAKE AND STRAIN INTO
A COCKTAIL GLASS
GARNISH: LIME WEDGE ON RIM

50ML MARTIN MILLER'S GIN
25ML LIME CORDIAL

TOM COLLINS

GLASS: HI-BALL
METHOD: SHAKE FIRST 3 INGREDIENTS
AND STRAIN INTO AN ICED FILLED HI-BALL.
TOP WITH SODA
GARNISH: LEMON PEEL

50ML MARTIN MILLER'S GIN
20ML LEMON JUICE
25ML SIMPLE SYRUP
SODA

*"People forget that many of today's famous vodka cocktails were originally made with gin.
Not just the Martini; The Bloody Mary was invented at Harry's New York Bar, Paris, and used
gin, but the guy who introduced it into the US thought the name too 'risque'
so changed it to the Red Snapper. Then there's the Southside, that's a Mojito with gin.
The list is endless. I call them my 'stolen cocktails'."*
MARTIN MILLER

THE STORY OF MARTIN MILLER'S GIN

GIN AND TONICS

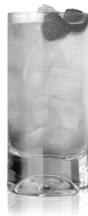

1915 G&T

GLASS: HI-BALL
METHOD: BUILD OVER CUBED ICE
IN GLASS
GARNISH: LEMON PEEL

50ML MARTIN MILLER'S GIN
SQUEEZE OF LEMON JUICE
GOOD QUALITY TONIC WATER
DASH OF ANGOUSTURA BITTERS

MILLER'S PIAZZA

GLASS: HI-BALL
METHOD: BUILD OVER CUBED ICE
IN GLASS
GARNISH: CUCUMBER SPIRAL

40ML MARTIN MILLER'S GIN
10ML CYNAR APERITIVO
DASH OF ORANGE BITTERS
GOOD QUALITY TONIC WATER

SAN SEBASTIAN G&T

GLASS: HI-BALL
METHOD: BUILD OVER CUBED ICE
IN GLASS
GARNISH: LEMON AND ORANGE PEEL

50ML MARTIN MILLER'S GIN
10ML FRESH ORANGE JUICE
10ML LEMON JUICE
DASH OF ORANGE BITTERS
GOOD QUALITY TONIC WATER

RASPBERRY G&T

GLASS: HI-BALL
METHOD: BUILD OVER CUBED ICE
IN GLASS
GARNISH: 2 RASPBERRIES

50ML MARTIN MILLER'S GIN
5ML RASPBERRY SYRUP
GOOD QUALITY TONIC WATER
SQUEEZE OF LIME

GIN TO NICKS

GLASS: HI-BALL
METHOD: BUILD OVER CUBED ICE
IN GLASS
GARNISH: LIME PEEL

50ML MARTIN MILLER'S GIN
DASH OF ANGOUSTURA BITTERS
SQUEEZE OF LIME JUICE
GOOD QUALITY TONIC WATER

"The simple G&T needn't be so simple. The basic ingredients of good quality, well balanced
gin and quality tonic water make a great starting point for some flair and creativity.
Try some of these variants on this great classic. They're a refreshing change from the
depressing 'ice and a slice' style G&Ts served in so many British bars and restaurants!"
MARTIN MILLER

MARTIN MILLER'S CLASSIC COCKTAILS

WALLIS BLUE	NEGRONI	FRENCH 75	AVIATION	RAMOS GIN FIZZ
GLASS: MARTINI *METHOD: SHAKE INGREDIENTS* *WITH CUBED ICE AND STRAIN INTO GLASS* *GARNISH: COAT RIM OF GLASS BY* *RUBBING WITH LIME SLICE* *AND DIPPING RIM IN SUGAR*	*GLASS: ROCKS* *METHOD: STIR IN ROCKS GLASS* *WITH CUBED ICE* *GARNISH: ORANGE SLICE*	*GLASS: FLUTE* *METHOD: SHAKE FIRST THREE INGREDIENTS,* *STRAIN INTO A FLUTE AND* *TOP WITH CHAMPAGNE* *GARNISH: LEMON TWIST*	*GLASS: MARTINI* *METHOD: SHAKE WITH CUBED ICE* *AND STRAIN* *INTO A COCKTAIL GLASS* *GARNISH: MARASCHINO CHERRY*	*GLASS: HI-BALL* *METHOD: SHAKE ALL INGREDIENTS* *WITH CUBED ICE,* *TOP WITH SODA* *GARNISH: NONE*
40ML MARTIN MILLER'S GIN *20ML COINTREAU* *20ML LIME JUICE* *DASH OF BLUE FOOD COLOURING*	*25ML MARTIN MILLER'S GIN* *25ML RED VERMOUTH* *25ML CAMPARI*	*20ML MARTIN MILLER'S GIN* *10ML LEMON JUICE* *15ML SIMPLE SYRUP* *TOP WITH CHAMPAGNE*	*50ML MARTIN MILLER'S GIN* *20ML LEMON JUICE* *20 MARASCHINO LIQUEUR*	*50ML MARTIN MILLER'S GIN* *10ML LIME JUICE* *10ML LEMON JUICE* *20ML SIMPLE SYRUP* *20ML CREAM* *DASH OF ORANGE BLOSSOM WATER* *TOP WITH SODA*

THE STORY OF MARTIN MILLER'S GIN

MARTIN MILLER'S CONTEMPORARY CLASSICS

NORTH SEA BREEZE

GLASS: HI-BALL
METHOD: BUILD IN HI-BALL GLASS
GARNISH: TWO LIME WEDGES

50ML MARTIN MILLER'S GIN
70ML FRESH PINK GRAPEFRUIT JUICE
70ML LYCHEE JUICE

BRAMBLE

GLASS: ROCKS
METHOD: BUILD IN GLASS
WITH CRUSHED ICE
GARNISH: BLACKBERRY

50ML MARTIN MILLER'S GIN
15ML SIMPLE SYRUP
5ML CRÈME DE MURE

WESTBOURNE PUNCH

GLASS: HI-BALL
METHOD: SHAKE FIRST FOUR INGREDIENTS
WITH ICE, STRAIN INTO ICE FILLED GLASS
AND TOP WITH SODA
GARNISH: GRAPEFRUIT SLICE AND MINT SPRIG

50ML MARTIN MILLER'S
WESTBOURNE STRENGTH GIN
20ML ST GERMAINE
20ML PINK GRAPEFRUIT JUICE
10ML LEMON JUICE
TOP WITH SODA

THE SAN FRANCISCO

GLASS: ROCKS
METHOD: SHAKE AND STRAIN INTO
AN ICE FILLED ROCKS GLASS
GARNISH: BLUEBERRIES
AND TARRAGON LEAVES

50ML MARTIN MILLER'S
WESTBOURNE STRENGTH GIN
15 ML LEMON JUICE
15ML SIMPLE SYRUP
12 BLUEBERRIES
6 TARRAGON LEAVES

TUSCAN SUNSET

GLASS: HI-BALL
METHOD: SHAKE ALL EXCEPT GINGER ALE,
STRAIN INTO AN ICE FILLED HI-BALL
AND TOP WITH GINGER ALE
GARNISH: MINT SPRIG

35ML MARTIN MILLER'S GIN
35ML ANTICA FORMULA VERMOUTH
15ML MARASCHINO LIQUEUR
20ML LIME JUICE
2 DASHES OF PEYCHAUDS'S BITTERS,
TOP WITH A GOOD QUALITY GINGER ALE

CREDITS AND THANKS

PHOTOGRAPHER DAVID ANGEL,
GETTY IMAGES,
JUPITER IMAGES,
TONY AT LORDPRICE,
SPLASH LONDON,
THE FARM.
MARTIN MILLER WOULD ALSO LIKE
TO THANK ALL OF HIS FRIENDS.
WITHOUT THEIR SUPPORT NONE
OF THIS WOULD HAVE BEEN
POSSIBLE.

FOR FURTHER INFORMATION OR CONTACT DETAILS
FOR MARTIN MILLER'S GIN WRITE TO:
THE REFORMED SPIRITS CO. LTD.,
PLAZA 535 KINGS ROAD,
LONDON SW10 0SZ

WWW.MARTINMILLERSGIN.COM

THE STORY OF MARTIN MILLER'S GIN